The Great Escape for Gamers

The Great Escape for Gamers

Table Of Contents

Foreword

People love gaming, and that's not always a disgusting thing. Whether played on a hand-held platform, a PC, or a TV, the games may supply hours of quiet fun. The games may advance PC skills and greater eye-hand coordination.

Video games are emotionally "untroubled." When a person makes an error, no one else sees (contrary to the public degradation of, say, striking out in a real world baseball game). And as every mistake made in gaming helps the player learn the specific action needed the next time, the player gets the satisfaction of steadily improving and finally winning.

All the same gaming bears a few downsides. Besides being truly expensive, many in demand games involve vivid sex and violence. Possibly most worrisome, they may be exceedingly habit-forming. Any person could become "addicted" to gaming, and people with AD/HD appear to be at specific risk.

Does the want to play video games rule your life? When the set has to be switched off, do you become mad? If so, the time has come to assist this yourself.

Gamer's Great Escape

Powerful Techniques For Quitting Gaming Addiction And Living The Good Life

Chapter 1:

Introduction To Your New Life

Synopsis

Why do you do it? You have to be able to settle that question. Is it to aid you in dealing with worries and stress? It may be difficult for you to acknowledge that you have a habit; however you can't shift what you don't acknowledge.

What purpose does the conduct serve for you? If you're a gamer, you're not merely playing because it's your job. Admit to yourself: I'm medicating myself for stress, depression and hurt. It numbs me to life.

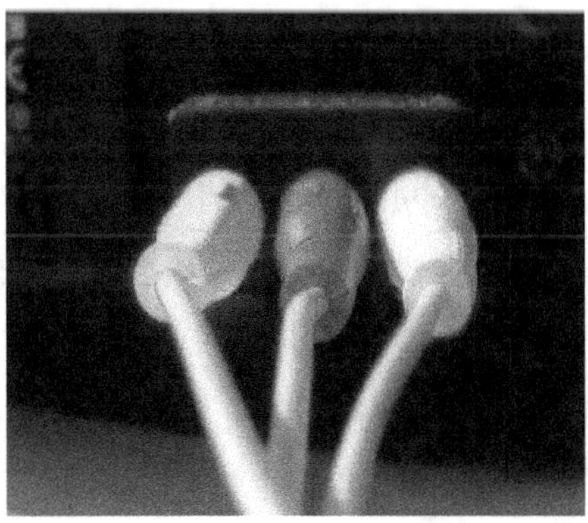

The Basics

There are any measure of reasons why somebody will deny that he or she has an addiction problem. Some causes have to do with embarrassment or concealment owed to true or perceived results (like getting penalized at home or suspended from school). A few people are humiliated that they have an issue that they feel that they can't control. They may feel bad about the things that they've done while focusing on the addiction.

There's also a lot of stigma affiliated with addiction. Being labeled a "addict" may have any number of social and psychological results for the addict, including lowering one's self-respect, limiting one's societal (e.g., being cut off from friends and loved ones), educational (i.e., being kicked out of school), or even occupational opportunities (e.g., not being employed at a local business).

A lot of times, People don't wish to admit that they've an addiction as it will mean being forced to abandon something that they value or something they require to get by. However there are true repercussions if you don't admit to having an issue. You may be subject to more examination by loved ones, friends, or People in the community that may result in societal consequences.

Also, many people believe they have their addiction "under control," however in most cases addictions gain command of you.

And occasionally an acquaintance, family member, or teammate is the one who encounters the signs of trouble first.

Triggers are mental and physical promptings that cause you to wish to gratify your addiction. Try and work out what kind of things makes you want to play video games. Possibly it's a certain site that you go to on the net that begins your video gaming hysteria.

Maybe it's being around certain People that make you hunger for a game or two. Do your best to figure out what sort of things make you wish to play games.

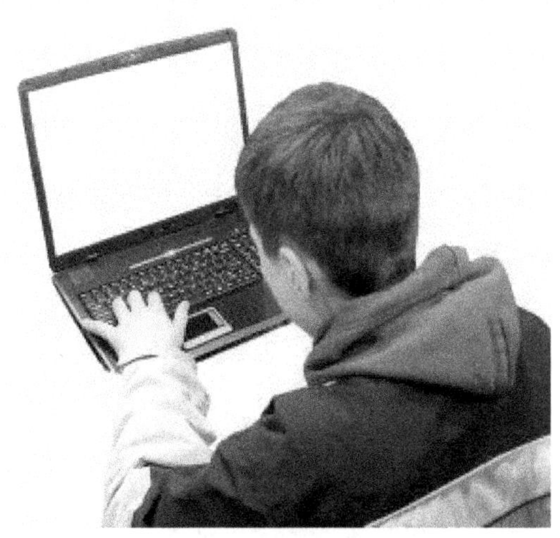

Chapter 2:

Synopsis

Affiliations between certain feelings, people, places, and things become entwined with the addict's conduct. If addicts find their way to change, the old affiliations between the addiction and the old feeling, people, places, and things live on, often setting off cravings to use and an OCD loop.

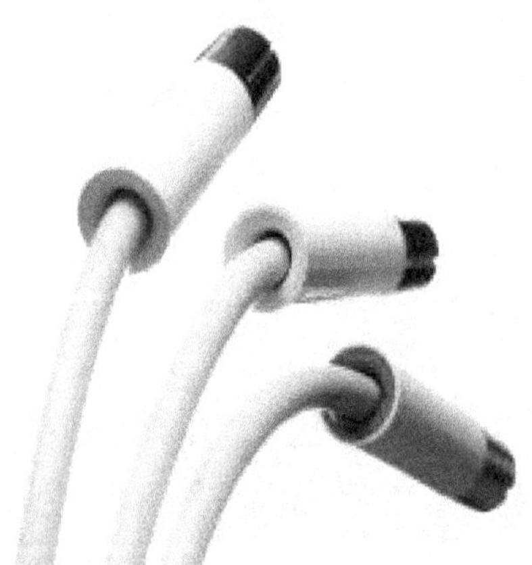

Changing It

If these cues set off memories and euphoric recall, you have to prevent cravings and possible backsliding. If you don't you remain exceedingly vulnerable to slipping on your change. These cues are ever present, but backsliding might be prevented.

It's crucial to avoid the external triggers that are your severest. Many of these will be the obvious ones like being around old gaming friends, or going to game shops.

Triggers that can't be kept away from altogether might be weakened. To be ready and able to weaken triggers that arise, you have to be able to anticipate and identify them, then have a plan of action on how you'll contend with them without using.

Below are areas that serve as things that might establish cravings to return to the addiction. Apply this to help identify your likely risks.

People

Who are the people you used to play video games with? Make a list. Make a list of others that might serve as a spark for backsliding. It may be extended loved ones, mate, girlfriend, your kids, boss, workfellows, neighbors and any others.

Areas

Where did you used to start getting the video game urge? What are the places that might set off cravings or euphoric recall? Make a list of the areas that may remind you of gaming/using or serve as spark. Instances might include: bars, school, work, certain streets, specific parts of town, particular rooms.

Things

What sorts of things did you routinely participate in while gaming? What are a few of the daily things that you may participate in now that might set off cravings?

Make a list of possible provoking things. Examples might include going to the game section of a shop, becoming bored, going gambling, going to gaming conventions, and others.

Discover other nerve-racking things or activities that may serve as a spark. Examples might include such matters as deaths of family, divorce, separation, cash issues, getting paid, getting a raise, unemployment, retiring, home alone, vacation, going by an ATM machine, home alone, etc..

What sorts of relationship things were affiliated with your gaming use? Differentiate relationship things that might serve as a spark. Examples may include meeting new people, leaving on a date, hanging out with friends, after arguing, prior to sex, following sex, family visits, separation, divorce, and so forth.

When did you generally use? Identify certain hours, week, month or year that might serve as a spark for backsliding. Examples might be Monday (Monday night football), Sunday (gearing up to go back to work), anniversary date or month of traumatic things, after work, prior to work, attempting to get to sleep, awakening in the night, and any other times that are crucial.

Making a plan.

- Looking back over your lists above, distinguish actions that you're able to take to cut back the threat to your recovery. What might you avoid?

- Which things or spots might you leave if you feel vulnerable? How may you empower yourself to leave?

- What may you do to shift how you think or feel if you find yourself in an inescapable position that's triggering a wish to use?

- Utilize thought stopping techniques to manage cravings if they happen.

  - ✓ Call somebody.
  - ✓ Call your counselor.
  - ✓ Engage someone who's supportive of your change in a conversation.

- ✓ Prompt yourself that cravings are temporary and that they'll go away if you don't use.
- ✓ Think that cravings are a regular part of change and that they don't destine you to failure.
- ✓ Remind yourself that you've the option whether you act on your cravings.

Consider a craving as a competition between you and your disease. Who will win?

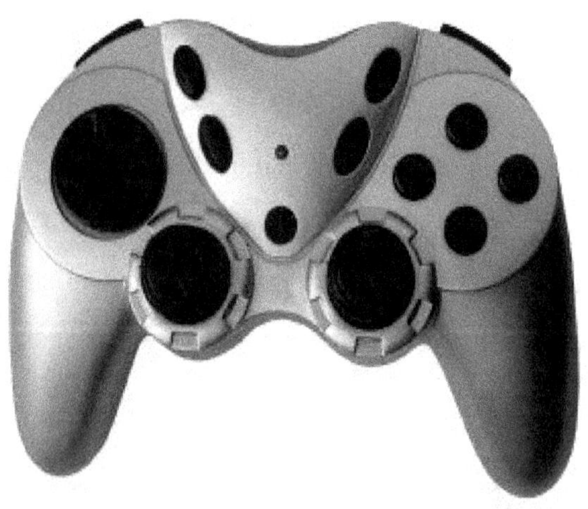

Chapter 3:
Alternative Entertainment Choices

Synopsis

An exceptional method for developing and beating addictions is to execute particular actions or activities, which you would rather avoid doing due to laziness, putting things off, weakness, shyness, etc..

By doing something that you don't like doing or are too lazy to accomplish, you overcome your subconscious resistance, school your brain to obey you, fortify your inner powers and gain inner strength. As well you could have some fun.

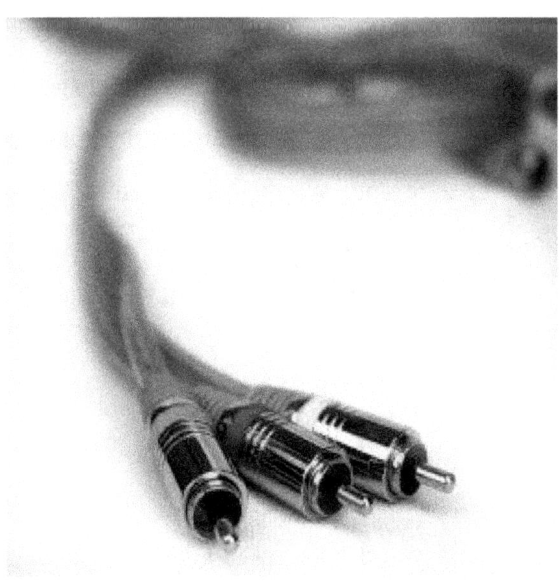

Something Else To Do

Muscles become stronger by resisting the power of weights. Inner strength is achieved by overpowering inner resistance.

Remember, fortifying one of these powers, automatically fortifies the other one. Here are a few tips:

Try being nice as an activity.

You're seated in a bus or train and an old man or woman, or a pregnant woman walks in. Stand and give up your seat even if you want to remain seated. Do this not only because it's polite, but as you're doing something that you're reluctant to do. In that way you're overcoming the resistance of your body, brain and feelings.

Get organized as an activity.

There are dishes in the sink that have to be washed and you postpone washing them for later. Get up and wash them right away. Don't let your laziness overcome you. When you recognize that in this way you're developing your self-discipline, and if you're convinced of the significance of self-control in your life, it will be simpler for you to do whatever you have to act.

Quit procrastinating as an activity.

You come home exhausted from work and sit in front of the television set, as you feel too lazy and fatigued to go and wash. Don't obey the want to just sit, but go and get a shower

Exercise for an activity.

You might recognize your body requires some exercise, but rather you keep on sitting doing nothing or watching a movie. Get up and walk, run or do a different exercise.

Exercise daily for thirty days. Abandon TV for thirty days. Get up at five daily for thirty days. Consider each 30-day test as a fun and intriguing challenge. You're merely conducting a test to determine if you like it.

Get motivated as an activity.

Overcome your laziness. Convince yourself of the importance of what is to be accomplished. Convince your brain that you gain inner strength when you act and accomplish things, despite laziness, reluctance or mindless inner resistance.

Get creative as an activity.

Finish an otherwise dull task in an uncommon or crazy manner to keep it fun and intriguing. Make routine calls utilizing fake foreign accents. Take notes in wax crayon. Experiment to find out how music might boost your effectiveness. Try trance or rock 'n' roll for e-mail, classical music for jobs, and complete silence for elevated concentration originative work.

If you practice weight lifting, running or aerobics, you fortify your muscles, so that when you have to move or carry something heavy for instance, you've the strength for it. By studying French daily, you'll be able to talk French if you visit France. It's the same with self-discipline and self-control; by strengthening yourself, all this becomes available for your use whenever you need it.

Most of these exercises might be practiced anywhere and at anytime, and you don't have to commit particular times for them. They'll train and grow your inner strength, enabling you to utilize it whenever you need it.

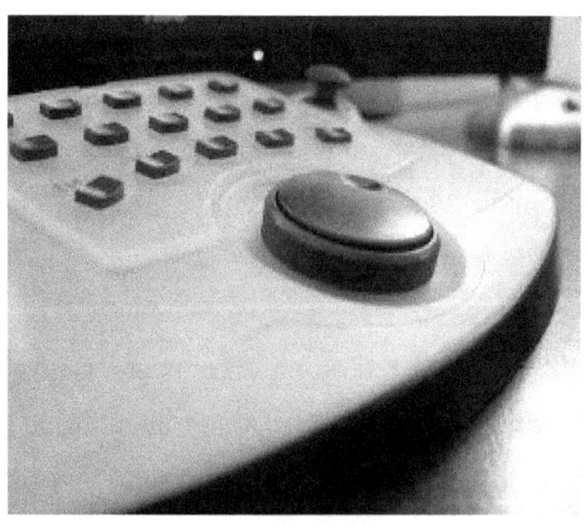

Chapter 4:

Why Go Social?

Synopsis

We know about the hurtful effects of playing video games. Well it's true that studies suggest that a firm diet of games may lead to asocial behavior. And this research, along with horse sense, is precisely why a lot of people down games.

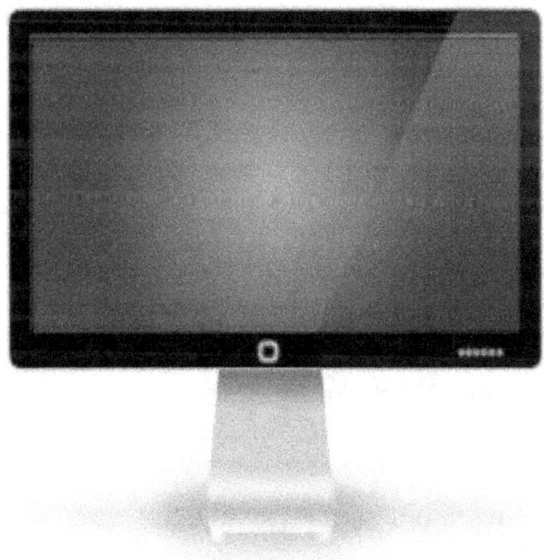

A Social Theme

The issue with this is that there is a more recent body of research that spotlights social benefits of gaming. And this research has a few crucial implications.

If playing games may lead to asocial behavior, it makes sense to suggest that playing prosocial games may lead to prosocial behavior. And research supports this proposition. For instance,

While these studies surely supported the hypothesis being tested in one study, the prosocial behavior being displayed was fairly trivial.

All the same, in a different experiment in a series of studies, the researchers found a much more powerful demonstration of this effect. In that study, players played a prosocial or neutral video game and were then exposed to a situation that really tested their willingness to help other people.

Specifically, the experimenters smartly staged an encounter in which a distressed ex-boyfriend walked into the lab during the experiment to face his ex-girlfriend who happened to be the experimenter.

Naturally, this was all part of the study; however to the player it seemed as if the experiment has simply been interrupted by a disgruntled ex-boyfriend. The ex-boyfriend ignored the players and began to harass the experimenter (his ex-girlfriend).

The results were pretty striking. 10 out of 18 players who had been playing the prosocial game stepped in to help the experimenter. Yet, only 4 out of the 18 players who had been playing the neutral game stepped in.

Put differently, several minutes of playing a silly but prosocial game in which you maneuver cute little animals safely to an exit seemed to increase the likelihood that individuals would stick their necks out for a stranger.

Why is this research significant? And why do we need more of it?
It's perhaps obvious as to why it was and is still significant to examine the potential neurological, psychological, and social effects of exposure to video games. It's likewise vital to more seriously examine the effects of socially positive gaming experiences.

1st, such research might further challenge the claim that video games are inherently asocial by demonstrating that it truly devolves on the game.

2nd, I think succeeding research needs to think about the fact that video games are increasingly complex, and not merely asocial or prosocial, violent or non-violent. Consider this. For the last couple of decades, despite the dangers and addictions, the popularity of video games has expanded.

There is an empirical link between violent gaming and belligerent thoughts and behavior. There are surely many games like this, but an increasing number of games with violent content center on adding moral dilemmas and social consequences.

Therefore, it's possible that the effects of video games on conduct are more complex than once thought.

Concisely, like all social influences, video games may be neutral, good, foul, and frequently a mix of all of the above. Games have been around for some time now and have become one of the most popular forms of amusement.

The main point being... if you have to play... make sure to play games and link up with social groups with themes that boost your social awareness.

Chapter 5:

Affirmations for Abstinence

Synopsis

All addictions might be dangerous and adverse to the addicted individual and other people around him; even so, video game addiction might be especially detrimental to youngsters.

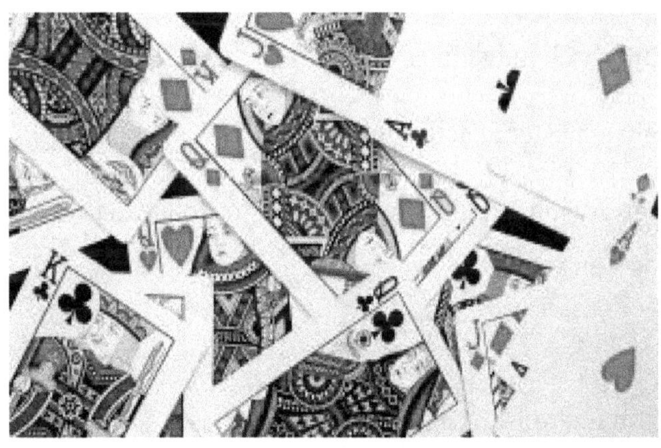

Some Help

Video games are becoming increasingly popular with youngsters of young ages, which in turn may raise the likelihood that these youngsters will develop addictions to video games.

What is more, playing violent games may be associated with a tendency to behave more aggressively, although the data is inconclusive about the cause and effect nature of this relationship.

Utilize affirmations to help.

- ✓ "I am self-asserting and persuasive in my life."

- ✓ "I approach individuals and engage them in conversations."

- ✓ "I am a master at achieving tasks."

- ✓ "I'm disciplined and self-reliant in following my addiction program."

Although numerous researchers advocate the position that video games induce violent behavior in youngsters and grownups, there are likewise many researchers who support the opposite belief, which is that video games purge one's want to act violently and thus cut down the amount of violence in which a person will engage.

Additional detrimental effects of video games include taking time away from studies or homework and diminished social skills. In the last analysis, despite possible detrimental effects of excessive video game playing, there are benefits to playing video games in moderation.

For instance, video games may improve spatial abilities, the ability to produce and apply multiple strategies, and may help develop critical analyzing techniques.

Due to the nature of video games, psychological, social, and neurological factors have all been affiliated with excessive video game playing.

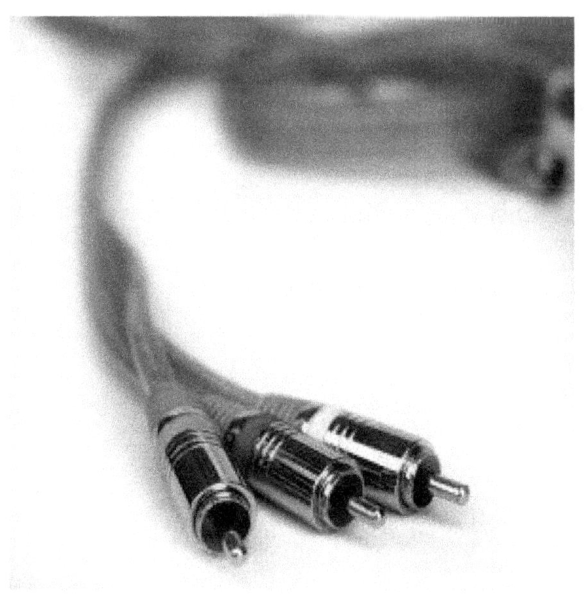

Chapter 6:

Tips For An Experiential Life

Synopsis

As a recovery plan, the addict should be monitored for video game usage. The addict ought to be rewarded and encouraged if doing well, and if seeing a counselor he should discuss why an addict did use if this does occur.

The addict and the counselor should discuss and together discover novel ways for the patient to solve life's issues and to make him happy, like meditating, working out, writing of song lyrics, volunteering or linking up with a support group.

The end goal is to have addicts become operational, responsible, and productive.

There are as well other fun things to do in life besides gaming:

Things To Think About

Here are some suggestions;

- ✓ Read

- ✓ Ride a bicycle

- ✓ Hike or walk around your neighborhood or city ("explore" your environment)

- ✓ Construct something

- ✓ Think over your future and figure out goals to get to it

- ✓ View TV or movies

- ✓ Check out the internet

- ✓ Workout/exercise

- ✓ Earn a trade (you could use the internet to assist you here...).

- ✓ Draw/paint

- ✓ Come up with your own song.

- ✓ Learn an instrument

- ✓ Study a new language

- ✓ Work out your interests and perhaps meet with someone to go over it

- ✓ Get a occupation

- ✓ Go to the store to check out the deals or something

- ✓ Clean your house

- ✓ Go through your storage and see if you still need that stuff

- ✓ Repair whatever needs repairing at your house

- ✓ Meet your neighbors if you haven't already

- ✓ Go to your city's site and check into what events are coming up

- ✓ Go to the movies

- ✓ Take pictures

- ✓ Spend a day someplace other than your house

A Potent way to get the ball rolling utilizing affirmations for optimum living is to write them down on an index card, and read it throughout the day. The more you practice them, the deeper the fresh beliefs will click. The best times to review your affirmations are first thing in the morning time, during the day, and prior to you retiring for the night.

Utilize affirmations while mediating. After relaxing into a deep, quiet, meditative state of mind, imagine that you've achieved health and wellness and know how to have optimum living. Imagine yourself in the physical setting or surroundings that you'd like, the house that you enjoy and find comforting, quieting your soul and receiving appreciation and appropriate recompense for your efforts. Add any additional details that are essential for you, like the physical things you wish to change, the amount of stress reduction to achieve, etc.

Try to get a feeling in yourself that this is possible; experience it like it was already happening. In short, imagine it exactly the way you'd like it to be, as if it were already so!

Try standing in front of a mirror and use affirmations while looking into your own eyes. If you can, repeat them out loud with passion. This is a powerful way to change your limiting beliefs very quickly.

If you discover it hard to believe an affirmation will occur, add "I select to" to the affirmation. "I select to have optimum living," for example, or, "I select to have less stress in my life."

Attach favorable emotions to your affirmations. Consider how accomplishing your goal will make you feel, or consider how good it feels to know that you're succeeding at optimum living. Emotion is a fuel which makes affirmations stronger.

If you find yourself merely parroting the words of your affirmations, rather than centering on their meaning, change affirmations. You're able to still affirm the same goals or features, naturally, but rephrasing your affirmations can regenerate their effectiveness.

Gratitude is a kind of affirmation: One that states the following: "I enjoy the health and wellness in my life and trust that more will come my way".

Wrapping Up

It's difficult to deny that a few individuals (whether they're youngsters, teens, or grownups) play video games far too much and that it may negatively impact their functioning and success outside from the glare of the monitor.

Naturally, not everybody becomes addicted to video games. Net games are enjoyed by millions of individuals around the world as a way to unwind, interact with acquaintances, and for simple entertainment uses.

All the same, it's becoming clear that there are those who lose control of their gaming habits.

Hopefully this book has given you tools to deal with this particular addiction.